Go Yogi!

A yogi is a person who practises yoga.

First published in 2017
by Singing Dragon
an imprint of Jessica Kingsley Publishers
73 Collier Street
London N1 9BE, UK
and
400 Market Street, Suite 400
Philadelphia, PA 19106, USA

www.singingdragon.com

Library of Congress Cataloging in Publication Data
A CIP catalog record for this book is available from the Library of Congress

British Library Cataloguing in Publication Data
A CIP catalogue record for this book is available from the British Library

ISBN 978 1 84819 341 3
eISBN 978 0 85701 297 5

Printed and bound in China

Go Yogi!

Everyday Yoga for Calm, Happy, Healthy Little Yogis

Written by
Emma Hughes

SINGING
DRAGON
LONDON AND PHILADELPHIA

Illustrated by
John Smisson

Namaste (said nam-as-tay) is an Indian way of saying hello and goodbye.

Yoga can help you feel healthy and happy.

We'll start with learning a special way of breathing, then a way to get our bodies nice and warm, and finally we'll share some of our favourite yoga poses.

It's good to practise yoga in a
space clear of toys and noise.

Sit with your legs crossed and
your back nice and tall.
Let's try a special yogi way of breathing...

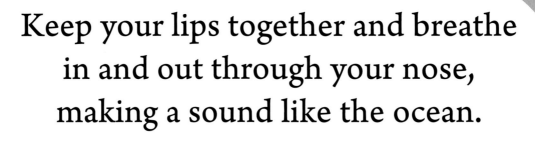

Keep your lips together and breathe
in and out through your nose,
making a sound like the ocean.

Sit here for a few moments,
listening to your breath.

Are you feeling calm?
Good, let's move on.

Grown-Up Yogi's Tip:
Encourage the child to sit nice and still,
taking 10 long breaths in and out.

Salute the Sun

Follow Flo as she practises steps 1–7.
Repeat the steps until you feel nice and warm.

Imagine the sun shining warm yellow light on your body.

Saluting the sun gets our bodies warmed up!

Grown-Up Yogi's Tip:
The sequence is great for memory and coordination. After a couple of rounds, see if the child can repeat the sequence by themselves.

Begin by standing tall. We call this Mountain Pose.

Take a deep breath in and reach your arms up high.

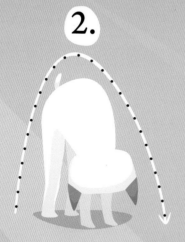

Lower your hands to the ground and say hello to your toes.

Step your legs back, lower your tummy to the ground.

4.

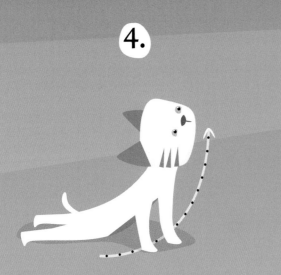

Shine your heart forward
and look up to the sky.

5.

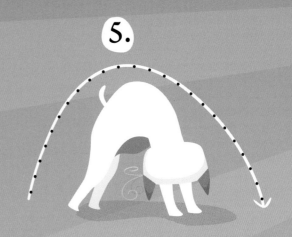

Root your hands and feet
into the ground and lift
your hips. Hold this
shape for 3–5 breaths.

6.

Step your legs towards
your hands.

7.

Reach up high, finishing
with your arms by your sides.

Check it out!

Now it's time to share some of
Mack and Flo's favourite yoga poses.

You don't have to practise them
all together – start with a few
and add more in when you're ready.

Mack and Flo show us how it's done.

Tea Pot

Step your legs apart, put your left hand on your waist and your right arm out to the side.

Turn your right foot so it's pointing in the same direction as your right hand. Now pour the tea!

The tipping is great for strengthening your waist. More tea anyone?

Grown-Up Yogi's Tip:
To move into the full pose, encourage the
child to lift their top arm and look towards it.

Don't forget to pour to the other side too,
everyone wants a cup.

Floating Feathers

Jump your feet wide apart and reach your arms towards the sky. Imagine your fingers are feathers, let your feathers gently float all the way to the ground.

Take a couple of breaths here, letting your feathers settle for a moment.

When we fold forward in our yoga practice, our senses, such as our hearing and vision, relax.

Grown-Up Yogi's Tip:

Encourage the child to inhale as they reach up and exhale as they fold forward, coordinating the breath with the movement.

Can you look at your feathers close up by gently lowering your head towards the ground?

Finish by floating your feathers back up to the sky.

Balancing Barn Door

Starting in Mountain Pose, lift one foot up and balance on one leg. Using the arm on the same side as your raised leg, hug your knee into your body.

Imagine your bent leg is a barn door. Open the barn door out to the side and hold it there for a few moments.

Inhale, bring the knee back to centre and lower the leg to the ground.

Brilliant for your balance!

Grown-Up Yogi's Tip:
Don't worry if your child wobbles or
loses their balance, encourage them to try again.

Don't forget to open the
barn door on the other side.

Cheeky Chair

From Mountain Pose, lift your arms above your head and imagine you're about to sit down.

Just as you go to take a seat, the cheeky chair moves away, so you're left hovering, in a lightning bolt shape.

Can you hold the shape for a couple of breaths?

The chair is cheeky, but it's making your legs really strong!

Grown-Up Yogi's Tip:

It's really common for the bottom to stick out. To prevent this, encourage the child to point their tummy button forward.

Warrior

Starting in Mountain Pose, step your right leg forward and bend your right knee.

Turn your left heel in and turn your upper body to the left.

Lift your arms and look towards your right hand.

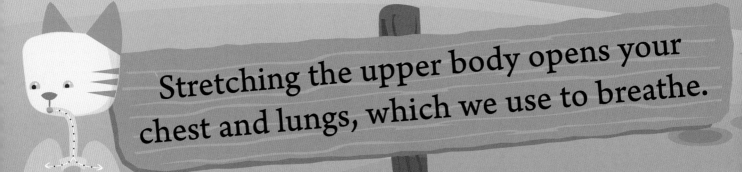

Stretching the upper body opens your chest and lungs, which we use to breathe.

Grown-Up Yogi's Tip:
Arms getting tired? Encourage the child to try practising the pose with hands on hips.

Take 5 long, deep breaths, feeling steady and strong. Don't forget the other side. No wonky Warriors here!

Balancing Boat

Sitting on your bottom, lift your legs up and lean back a little.

Ride the waves by rolling onto your back for just a moment, then breathe in and bring your boat back up to your balancing position.

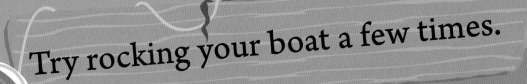

Try rocking your boat a few times.

Grown-Up Yogi's Tip:
To prevent hunching of the shoulders, encourage the child to lift their chest and roll their shoulders back.

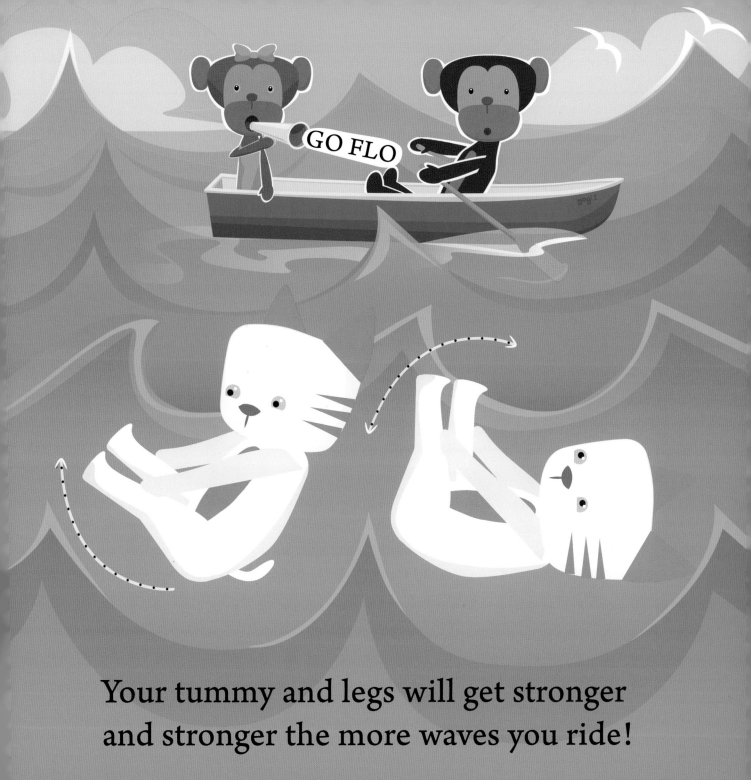

Your tummy and legs will get stronger
and stronger the more waves you ride!

Pebble on the Shore

Kneel on the floor, touching your big toes together, and sit on your heels.

Lower your head to the ground and let your arms relax by your sides.

Feel peaceful in your pebble pose.

Grown-Up Yogi's Tip:
This is a resting pose that can be used at any time; after a challenging yoga pose or after a challenging moment in the day.

Take some nice, long breaths in and out.
Breathe in and count 1, 2, 3, 4.
Breathe out and count 1, 2, 3, 4.

Imagine you're a pebble on the shore and your
deep breaths are the waves gently washing over
you. Each wave makes you a shinier pebble.

Butterfly

Sit up straight and bring your heels
together to create your wings.

Flap your wings like a butterfly.
Can your wings touch the ground?

Your flittering fluttering butterfly
wings are great for your hips.

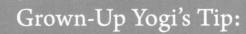

Grown-Up Yogi's Tip:

The child could finish this pose by folding forward and lowering the
chest towards the ground. Forward folds are relaxing to the senses.

Tick Tock Clock

Sit with your feet wide apart.
Breathe in and lift both of your arms high.
As you breathe out, lower your arms to your
left leg, then centre, then to the right leg and
then back up again.

Imagine your arms are the hands
of a clock – tick, tock, tick, tock.

Can you go anti-clockwise too?

Grown-Up Yogi's Tip:

Only straighten the legs if it feels comfortable, bent knees are fine.

Imagine time standing still as you take a pause with your arms in the centre position and lower your head toward the ground in front of you.

Calming Candle

Lie on your back and lift your bottom and legs up.

Put your hands on your back to help keep you up.

Imagine you're a candle and your feet are the flickering flame.

Being upside-down helps move blood around our bodies, is great for our hearts and makes us feel relaxed.

Grown-Up Yogi's Tip:
To encourage a straight line from the legs to the spine, lightly take hold of the child's legs and give them a gentle lift up.

Resting Yogi

Now for Mack's favourite bit – it's time for a rest.

Lie back on your mat and let your whole body go floppy. Take a deep breath into your tummy, then release all the air through your mouth and make a 'Ha' sound.

haaaaaaaaaaa

Grown-Up Yogi's Tip:
To help the child relax, you could read from their favourite book, play a piece of gentle music or repeat a positive mantra.

That should feel really good,
do it again if you like.

Close your eyes and try to be still. There's
nothing to think about and nothing to do. Bliss!

Lovely Lotus

Our yoga practice is finished for the day, but we can always come back to our Lovely Lotus seat whenever we need time out.

Just sit still, close your eyes and breathe. Namaste, Yogis.

Namaste (said nam-as-tay) is an Indian way of saying hello and goodbye.

Grown-Up Yogi's Tip:
To prevent slouching, ask the child to imagine there's a piece of string at the top of their head, lifting them up.

Grown-Up Yogi's Notes

Yoga has been around for thousands of years. Originating in India, yoga is practised for its physical, emotional and spiritual benefits.

Introducing yoga at an early age provides children with some useful tools to help them through times of worry, anxiety or chaos.

Yoga gives 'time-out' from the technology-focused, pressurised time we live in.

Yoga is beneficial for all children, but especially for those who experience anxiety, low self-esteem or diagnoses such as ADHD. Yoga will help children who are easily distracted become more 'present'.

By focusing on the movement of the body and the breath, yoga gives our busy brains a break, making the practice great for improving concentration and memory.

The aim of this book is to engage young children with yoga, so they might continue a practice throughout their lives and enjoy the many benefits yoga brings.

Flo and Mack introduce three stages of physical yoga practice: how to tune into the breath, how to practise sun salutations (to get the body warmed up) and a variety of asanas (poses) that children will enjoy mastering.

The poses given in this book are taken from the Ashtanga Yoga system and have been modified for younger yogis.

Encourage children to listen to their bodies and only practise what feels good. If a pose feels uncomfortable, ask them to come out of the pose – you can always try again another day.

It's best to practise yoga in a clear, quiet space, free of distractions. If you have a yoga mat, great, if not, a towel or blanket works just fine.

Turn off your phone, put the 'to-do' list to one side, breathe and enjoy.

Emma Hughes

Emma is an Ashtanga Yoga teacher and
has practised yoga for some 20 years.
She is a mum and a volunteer mentor, working with
vulnerable young people in her home city of Bath.

John Smisson

John is an artist, currently specialising in graphical
illustration for children. John's roots are in Fine Art,
but more recently has moved his focus
to digital art and design.